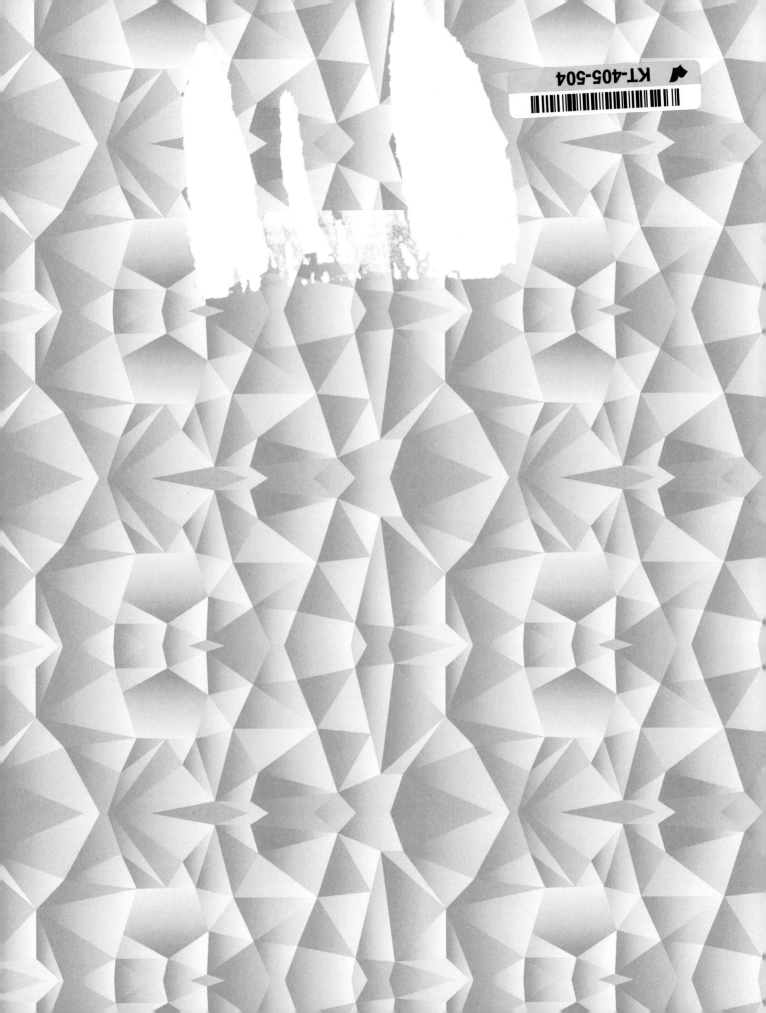

big
brands

SAMSUNG

Cath Senker

WAYLAND

contents

A global brand – Samsung today   **4**

Samsung starts out   **6**

The global arena   **8**

A new management style   **10**

Creating a market for electronics   **12**

Building the Samsung brand   **14**

Samsung v Sony   **16**

18 Overcoming recession and scandal

20 Sponsorship

22 The consumer culture

24 The secrets of Samsung's success

26 Samsung's future

28 Market a new Samsung product

30 Glossary and Further information

32 Index

A global brand: Samsung today

Have you looked in a phone shop recently? If you glanced at the latest smartphones, you probably spotted a few Samsungs.

The Samsung Galaxy S, one of the company's high-end smartphones.

The brand is well known for its classy mobiles – in 2013, one-third of smartphones bought worldwide were Samsungs! Samsung has introduced us to futuristic devices, such as the ultra-high-definition TV with its curved screen, and the Gear S Smartwatch, a slim, wearable smartphone with a keyboard, navigation system, music player and personal fitness monitor. Samsung leads the world in the development of graphene, the super-thin touchscreen material of the future.

In 2014 Samsung was the world's largest electronics and information technology (IT) company for the fourth year running. As well as smartphones, it makes all kinds of electronics and components, including TVs and memory chips. Based in South Korea, the company is also involved in skyscraper and plant construction, fashion, medicine, finance, and the petrochemical and hotel industries. In 2013, its revenue reached around US $216 billion (£135 billion) – more than rival tech companies HP, Siemens and Apple.

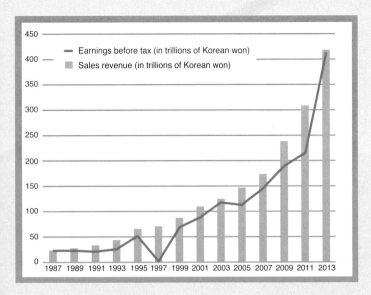

In 2013 Samsung was ranked eighth in Interbrand's list of the world's most valuable brands. Samsung's excellent product designs are key to its success; it won nine design awards in 2013. The brand is also known for new innovations – it has clocked up some world 'firsts', such as WiBro, the first mobile broadband technology. Because the brand is so powerful, Samsung is able to charge premium prices. It sells its TVs, mobiles and memory chips at higher prices than most of its competitors.

This book looks at how Samsung developed from a South Korean manufacturer of sugar, wool and chemicals to become one of the top global electronics companies. What allowed it to become the market leader in producing memory chips? How did it overtake its rival Sony, and manage to create smartphones to rival Apple's best-selling iPhones? What enables it to stay ahead of its competitors and how likely is it to remain at the top of the fiercely competitive electronics market?

Business Matters
Brand value

Indications of brand value include how well branded products sell, and the role of the brand in the decision to buy them.

The Samsung Gear S smartwatch lets you use your phone hands-free.

Samsung starts out

In the early years, Samsung sold groceries.

Samsung was founded as a food export company by ambitious Korean business-man Byung-Chull Lee in 1938. In the mid-1950s, after the Korean War (1950–53) left the country divided into North and South Korea, Samsung became a major corporation. It manufactured sugar, flour, woollen fabric and chemical fibres, and sold financial services. In 1961, a military (army-run) government took power in South Korea. It supported Samsung's growth because it was good for building up the poor economy. Byung-Chull became the richest man in South Korea.

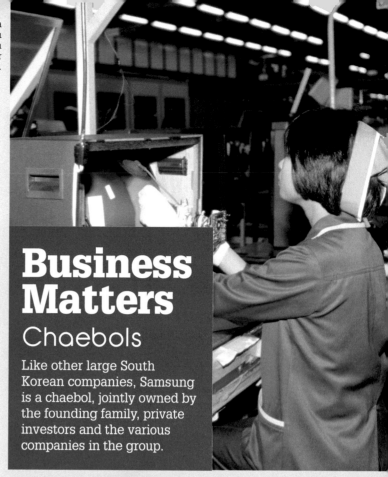

orking at the
msung Electronics
ctory in the 1980s.

Assembling a
Samsung TV in
1987; TV production
was a key area for
the company.

Byung-Chull Lee
Founder of Samsung

Byung-Chull Lee founded Samsung on the Japanese model. As Chief Executive Officer (CEO), he was the 'father' of the company, the employees were his 'family', and there was harmony between them. Workers had a job for life and the longer they worked for the company, the higher their salary. This management model was later adapted to better suit the changing business environment.

Business Matters
Chaebols

Like other large South Korean companies, Samsung is a chaebol, jointly owned by the founding family, private investors and the various companies in the group.

In 1969 Byung-Chull Lee moved into the expanding electronics industry, founding Samsung Electronics and Sanyo-Samsung Electronics as part of the Samsung Group. Much of the technology, including the components, came from Japan, but from 1973–4, oil prices quadrupled, damaging economies worldwide. Japan cut back much of its investment in Korea.

Byung-Chull decided Samsung would manufacture its own components and took over Korea Semiconductor, which produced silicon chips. (There are two kinds of chips: the microprocessor, which has the instructions for computer programs, and the memory chip, which holds programs and information.) Samsung made great strides in the industry, and in 1983 developed a high-speed memory chip. By now, it was South Korea's top company.

> "Samsung's research lab... reminded me of a dilapidated [run-down] high-school science classroom. But the work going on there intrigued me. They'd gather color televisions from every major company in the world... and were using them to design a model of their own."

Ira Magaziner, a US business consultant who visited Samsung Electronics in 1977

the global arena

In 1987, the military government in South Korea finally came to an end. Under the new government, people became better off, and were eager to buy Samsung TVs, video recorders and washing machines. Samsung also developed chemical, genetic engineering and aircraft industries.

Kun-Hee Lee, who took over as Samsung's chairman in 1987, was not content with owning South Korea's biggest company; he wanted Samsung to be a global leader. To rise to the challenge, he attempted to change the management style, encouraging young staff to join and to develop their own ideas. But senior managers who had worked at Samsung for many years resisted change. They wanted the juniors to obey instructions, and were obsessed with increasing sales rather than developing new products.

Kun-Hee decided on a fresh approach. Samsung would focus on its semiconductor industry, which required huge investment in equipment, technology and expert staff. It presented an ideal opportunity to shift the way the business operated. In 1992, Samsung Electronics achieved its first important success, becoming the world's leading company in semiconductors. It developed the world's first 64MB DRAM, the most common form of random access memory (RAM) for computers.

Chairman Kun-Hee Lee focused on company strategy and left day-to-day decisions to his managers.

Samsung Aerospace was involved in the development of Lockheed Martin's F-16 fighter aircraft from 1997 to 2004.

Yet the Samsung Group's home appliances weren't doing as well. They achieved high sales in South Korea, but were not in the first rank globally. In 1993, Kun-Hee watched a programme on Samsung's in-house TV network and was appalled to see workers sawing washing machine lids by hand to make them fit properly. The products simply weren't good enough.

Building the brand
PR stunts

A dramatic PR stunt can draw attention to a business and change its image. In 1995, Samsung gave 2,000 cordless phones to its employees as a New Year gift. When many complained about the poor quality of the devices, Kun-Hee was furious. He asked them to bring back the phones, and recalled poor-quality car phones and fax machines too. Workers at the Samsung factory in Gumi, wearing headbands saying 'Ensure quality', smashed up the faulty goods and set fire to them. This was Kun-Hee's message to the world that Samsung was determined to do better.

Jong-Yong Yun

Samsung Electronics Chief Executive Officer (CEO), 1996–2008

Jong-Yong Yun steered Samsung through its most difficult decade. In 1998, he cut the company's debt by US $13 billion (£8 billion) in one year by selling off failing businesses, made operations more efficient and cut costs. Jong-Yong Yun pushed for Samsung to embrace digital technology and produce high-quality consumer electronics, such as mobile phones. He encouraged improved communications among the workforce by giving all staff notebook computers and mobiles.

a new management style

In 1993, Chairman Kun-Hee revealed his New Management Initiative to make Samsung a dominant global company. He switched the company's focus from the quantity to the quality of the goods produced.

Kun-Hee introduced elements of the US business model. Staff now earned a salary based on their performance, rather than how long they had worked for Samsung. Instead of vertical communication alone, from managers down to juniors, he encouraged horizontal communications among skilled workers at the same level. Everyone had to believe 'change begins with me'. Kun-Hee also fostered a sense of crisis to keep everyone on their toes, foretelling that 'All of Samsung's number-one products will disappear in 5 or 10 years'. He pushed the company to adapt to change.

In 1997, an economic crisis hit East Asia. Samsung sold off unprofitable businesses and cut the workforce, which was considered a very 'un-Korean' thing to do. Yet to push the business forward, it offered generous salaries to talented new staff, often from abroad.

A worker carrying a placard bearing the face of Kun-Hee Lee at a protest about job losses at Samsung in 1998.

A worker at Samsung's factory in Cikarang, Indonesia in 2006.

Samsung made huge investments in the research and development (R&D) of new products, picking areas that it hoped would be popular – mobiles, flat-panel computer monitors and memory chips. The company had been behind in producing analogue devices but now it focused on new digital technologies. Entering the digital technology market early enabled the company to get ahead of its competitors. Overall, the strategy was successful, and Samsung emerged stronger than ever.

Business Matters
Research and development (R&D)

Companies carry out R&D to find new products and processes or to improve existing ones.

> **My co-workers spend a lot of time discussing each other's ideas to help each other develop them further.**
>
> Wesley Park, Samsung manager, 2005

	Samsung's growth stages		Major events at Samsung
1938–mid-1950s	Foundation and establishment of Samsung's management system	Small and middle-sized company (foundation and formation of core businesses)	Entry into manufacturing (1953–1954)
Mid-1950s–late 1960s	Growth into a large company	Large company (initial stage as a business group)	Diversification (electronics, heavy industry and chemicals)
Late 1960s–late 1980s	Emerges as S. Korea's leading company	Large business group	Start of the semiconductor business
Late 1980s–present	Emerges as a world-class company	Global business group	New Management initiative (1993) Restructuring (late 1990s) Global number-one products (in electronics, shipbuilding, heavy industry and chemicals)

Building the brand
Investing in manufacturing

Electronics companies succeeded in creating a market for their products. But there were many competing companies. How did Samsung stay ahead of the game? It developed the lead in a specialist area: memory chips. Samsung's huge investment in manufacturing facilities for memory chips allowed it to widen the gap with its rivals. Whatever new products were developed, they would require chips, and Samsung was the world leader, able to produce them in massive quantities.

In 1999, workers in a factory near Seoul make Samsung's latest product, the notebook computer.

…o recorders (VCRs) are
…mbled at Samsung Electronics in
…9. VCRs allowed people to record
…programmes, a new innovation.

Creating a market for electronics

Abig challenge for companies producing goods using new technologies is creating a market for them. In the late 20th century, how did Samsung and other electronics companies persuade people to buy products they had never needed before?

Timing was key. Samsung Electronics was set up at the perfect moment. The supply of electricity was growing in South Korea in 1969. Koreans saw that people in the West had TVs, fridges and fans, and they wanted them too. Samsung successfully exploited the availability of electricity to provide products that used it.

Likewise, Samsung's move into producing the semiconductors used in microprocessors was well timed. The development of microprocessors enabled computers to be made much smaller, in larger quantities and far more cheaply than before. In the 1980s, these personal computers (PCs) were marketed to businesses. Companies such as Microsoft created software applications for businesses, including word-processing programs and spreadsheets for doing accounts. Bill Gates, the co-founder of Microsoft, talked of a future where there would be 'a computer on every desk'. This prediction proved true, and soon computers were an essential business tool.

From the mid-1990s, the Internet took off in wealthy countries, and now people wanted to have PCs for entertainment as well as work. The price of computers fell further, and electronics companies pushed for everyone to have a computer at home. At this time, Samsung was a main supplier of computer components.

Business Matters
Advertising

When companies develop new technologies, they invest heavily in advertising to sell them. Computer companies were extraordinarily successful; the number of computers sold rose from 50,000 in 1975 to 134.7 million in 2000.

Computers have transformed publishing: here, old books are scanned so that people can read them on a website.

13

Samsung's stand at a trade fa[ir]
Las Vegas promotes the world's
curved Ultra High Definition [TV]

building the Samsung brand

A visitor examines Samsung's brand-new flat-screen monitor at a trade show in the USA, 1996.

Chairman Kun-Hee was determined to push the Samsung brand to the top. From the 1990s, he planned a global marketing campaign to make Samsung a household name in the West.

Samsung switched from making functional basics to focusing on high-value goods – items that consumers wanted on an emotional level. From 1995, it created desirable mobiles and flat-panel LCDs, which were lighter and more energy efficient than the older screens. This was Samsung's new premium-brand strategy. Would it work?

Samsung's head of marketing, Eric Kim, ran a test campaign in the USA in 2001, followed by a huge global marketing campaign. The company broke links with discount stores such as Wal-Mart in the USA and made new alliances with high-end independent stores, such as Best Buy and Sears. Customers started linking Samsung with quality goods. The company also tapped into the appeal of convergence products – devices with many electronic functions, such as colour LCD mobiles and wireless handheld PCs. These moves succeeded in changing Samsung's image from an unfashionable South Korean brand to a popular company producing must-have items to rival Apple's sleek computers and iPods.

Building the brand
Price skimming

From 2001, Samsung decided to go for a policy of price skimming – setting a relatively high price to boost profits. Well-known businesses frequently do this when they launch a new, premium-quality product. If consumers want the latest model, they'll be prepared to pay the price.

> It was a change in 1996 by our chairman, who wanted to build a brand, not just a product… We looked to the future to build the Samsung brand as iconic – one that everybody would want to have.

Gregory Lee, Global Chief of Marketing, 2005

Business Matters
Economy pricing

If you sell a product at a low price, more people may be eager to buy it; however, they may also think it's a poor-quality item. Also, you will make less profit per product sold and have less money to invest in the company.

Samsung

Eric Kim achieved his aim for Samsung to beat Sony within five years; he then resigned to take up a less stressful job.

Samsung opted to raise its brand image by going head to head with its major competitor, Sony. In 2000, Japanese company Sony was Samsung's biggest rival in DRAMs, electronic appliances and mobiles. Founded around the same time as Samsung, Sony was near the top of the electronics league; only Matsushita and Philips had higher sales. In 2000, its sales were US $70 billion (£44 billion) – more than double Samsung's US $28 billion (£17 billion). But Sony's growth had slowed to 5% per year while Samsung was expanding at a super-fast 25%.

In 2001, Eric Kim announced Samsung intended to overtake Sony within five years, and his goal hit the headlines around the world. The battle was on!

SONY

Sony

South Koreans are extremely hard workers, and the contest with Sony inspired workers at Samsung's main Suwon campus to work harder than ever. As well as mobiles, Samsung created portable DVD players and high-definition-ready LCD TVs – items that consumers bought because they were enticing rather than essential. Its products flew out of the shops. Market experts commented that by 2003, 'young consumers were ogling Samsung cell phones [mobiles] and flat-panel TVs the way their parents once lusted after Sony products'. Two years later, in 2005, Samsung had a higher brand value than Sony.

However, in 2007, business growth worldwide slowed down. Samsung's fantastic growth rate faltered and profits fell. The company faced a fresh crisis.

Eric Kim
Head of Global Marketing, 1999–2004

Korean-American Eric Kim pushed for Samsung to sell products at a higher price. The contest with Sony was also his brainchild. In 2001, Kim came up with the DigitAll campaign. At that time, people in most countries believed that digital technology was just for wealthy users. Kim stressed that Samsung's digital technology could meet everyone's needs – both business and personal – and that investing in its products was worthwhile. This was already true in South Korea, where most people had advanced digital mobiles and internet broadband access was the highest in the world. But it was a revolutionary idea in the USA.

17

overcoming
recession&

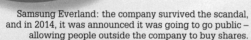

Business Matters
Relocation

Wages are an enormous expense for every company. To cut costs, multinational companies frequently move their factories to countries where wages are lower; in Vietnam in 2007, workers earned around one-tenth of the pay of South Korean workers.

Samsung Everland: the company survived the scandal, and in 2014, it was announced it was going to go public – allowing people outside the company to buy shares.

scandal

Samsung lost no time in adopting measures to survive the economic crisis. In 2007, Kun-Hee Lee announced restructuring (company reorganization) and cost-cutting plans. The company moved its main mobile production facilities from South Korea to Vietnam, where labour costs were much lower.

Samsung was hit by another crisis in 2008 – a political scandal. Kun-Hee Lee had begun to transfer his wealth to his son, Jae-Yong Lee, who was a major shareholder in Samsung Everland, South Korea's largest amusement park. In 2007, two directors of Everland were convicted for corrupt practices. They had sold Everland shares to Jae-Yong Lee at less than half the market value (which was illegal). The case damaged Samsung's good reputation, and Kun-Hee was forced to resign. However, he became chairman again two years later.

Samsung overcame this scandal, and the company survived and thrived during the 2008 global economic crisis. Its market share of mobile handsets rose from 16 to 21 per cent in one year, and it grabbed market share from Nokia and Sony Ericsson, keeping its high position despite the introduction of Apple's extremely popular iPhone in 2008. Samsung maintained its lead in producing components, and was a brand that people wanted to own. It focused on its digital convergence strategy – integrating voice, text and images on one device. For example, the 2012 Galaxy camera had a wireless connection so people could instantly upload their photos to share.

Building the brand
Diversification – widening the product range

Big businesses prefer to spread their risks. Realizing that the electronics industry might not continue to prove profitable, Kun-Hee sought new avenues for business in the 2010s. Samsung diversified into new industries, including biotechnology, pharmaceuticals and medical equipment, and invested heavily in biosimilars, which are cheaper versions of brand-name biotechnology drugs. The company does nothing by halves; it aimed to become the principal pharmaceutical company in the world!

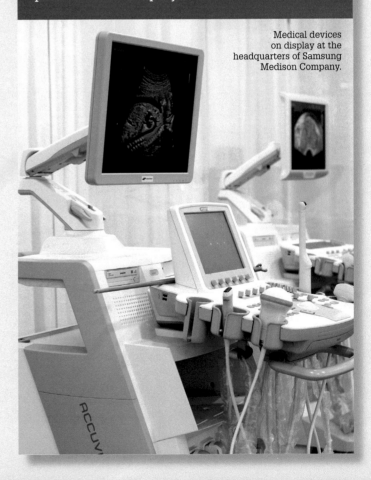

Medical devices on display at the headquarters of Samsung Medison Company.

Sponsorship

Top companies queue up to sponsor popular sports competitions to raise the profile of their business and encourage people to link their brand with these exciting events.

From 1998, Samsung became the official sponsor of communications equipment for the Olympic Games, providing wireless communications. Using the Olympics global brand proved ideal for pushing the company worldwide. After the Sydney Olympic Games in 2000, Samsung was placed second in the world after Coca-Cola in brand awareness ranking.

From 2006, Samsung sponsored the Paralympics to build its brand image, as well as other sports. It secured a deal to sponsor the shirts for English football team Chelsea from 2012–15 – every shirt worn by a team member or fan had the name Samsung emblazoned large on the front.

Samsung uses adverts based on Olympics themes in many markets around the world. For London 2012, football star David Beckham was the face of Samsung's Olympics advertising campaign, Everyone's Olympic Games. It spread the message that TV was no longer the main way to enjoy the Olympics. People could watch the games and share their favourite moments immediately on their new Samsung Galaxy phone, with special mobile apps that allowed them to play 3D and augmented reality sports games with their friends.

The Samsung Olympic Games sponsor lorry accompanies the Olympic torch relay through the British streets.

Business Matters

Building brand affection

Companies look for ways to contribute to society to build affection for their brand. In 2014, Samsung funded the TV programme Launching People in several countries. This recruited celebrities from the food, film, music and photography worlds to mentor budding cooks, film directors, photographers and musicians. The programme featured Samsung tablets, phones and cameras and aimed to show how Samsung technology could help talented people to achieve their dreams.

The launch of Everyone's Olympics Games in London, with David Beckham and athlete Zara Phillips.

> **Consumers are spending about eight minutes per visit on average on 'How Olympic Are You?'. This is double the time they spend on ordinary Samsung sites.**
>
> Ralph Santana, Samsung's Chief Marketing Officer, notes the popularity of Samsung's Olympics-themed webpages in 2012.

Electronic scrap at a recycling yard. In the USA, just 29 per cent of electronic waste was recycled in 2012.

Business Matters

Planned obsolescence

Electronics companies tend to design products with a limited life so people often have to replace them. For example, software is constantly changing, so if you have an old computer, you can't install the latest software on it. The operating system may no longer be supported with security updates so you are prone to computer viruses.

the consumer culture

Singer, and Samsung ambassador, Lily Allen.

Building the brand
Targeting the youth market

In 2014, Samsung targeted the youth market for mobiles in the UK, using singer Lily Allen to market its new premium handset, the Galaxy Alpha. It aimed to show the smartphone being used by what it called 'Alpha Britons'. According to Samsung, these were young people who 'embody the spirit of new modern Britain and its stylish youth culture.' The marketing campaign was timed to compete with Apple's iPhone 6, which was released at the same time.

Do you really need a new phone each time an upgrade comes out? Mobiles have become a vital accessory, and electronics companies have persuaded many people that it's best to have the newest version with the latest features.

Businesses use social media networks to entice consumers to purchase new products. Samsung has had huge success on Facebook, promoting its major product launches to reach 25 million fans in Europe in 2013. As well as providing information about its devices, it promotes two-way communication with fans, who can share their stories about Samsung purchases. This enables the company to pick up on any problems with its new releases and address them quickly.

The culture of constantly renewing our electronic gadgets has a cost to the environment though – we create mountains of electronic waste, much of it containing toxic materials. Many materials can be reclaimed and recycled, but this takes money and resources. Samsung is trying to clean up its act. In 2012, it was 7th in the Greenpeace Guide to Greener Electronics. It is a leader in providing warranties and spare parts information to help extend product lifetimes. Yet few people use their gadgets for the full lifespan.

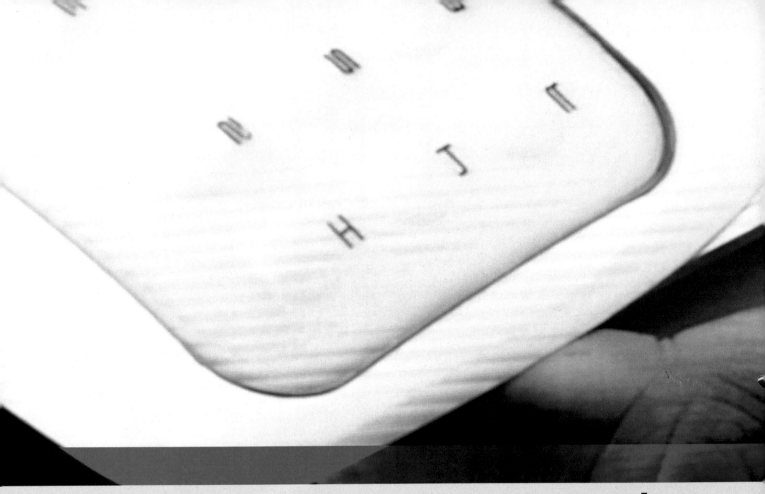

the secrets of Samsung's success

The Samsung booth at an electronics show in Las Vegas, USA in 2014.

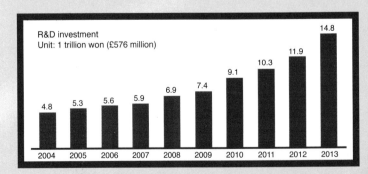

R&D investment
Unit: 1 trillion won (£576 million)

2004	2005	2006	2007	2008	2009	2010	2011	2012	2013
4.8	5.3	5.6	5.9	6.9	7.4	9.1	10.3	11.9	14.8

Dong-Hoon Chang, Executive Vice-President of Samsung Electronics, speaks at a digital technology meeting, 2013.

Business Matters

Co-opetition

Samsung has coined the term 'co-opetition' – a mixture of competition and cooperation – to describe how it expects its employees to work. Businesses within the Samsung Group have to compete to outperform each other and compete with outside suppliers to deliver parts and materials. Yet each division has to create innovative products, so employees have to cooperate together within their teams.

How does Samsung stay ahead of its competitors? In Korea, ppali ppali (quickly, quickly) is a common saying. Samsung has adopted the ppali ppali spirit, bringing out products faster than its rivals. In the mid-2000s, Japanese companies took an average of ten months to plan and release camera mobiles, while Samsung completed the same process in half the time. The speed of production forms an essential part of the brand's message: if you want the latest innovation, buy Samsung.

The company is able to churn out new products speedily through 'leapfrog' R&D. While it is designing a product, employees are already working on the next-generation, the next-next generation and even the one after that!

Production is fast because Samsung has its division headquarters (control centre), major R&D and manufacturing facilities in South Korean cities that are all within a radius of 30 km (18 miles) of each other. The core parts of the Samsung Galaxy S5 phone are all made within the Samsung Group. Having all the sites close together allows for good communications between the different divisions and a fast decision-making process. Experts from the R&D teams meet with the engineers from the manufacturing plant to discuss production issues, resolve any problems and make changes straight away.

From 2000, Samsung set out to lead the market in innovation – each company and division was expected to create a novel product. To foster creativity, it has Creative Labs (C-Labs) and a Creative Academy to encourage employees to come up with new ideas. On 'C-Lab days', they demonstrate the results of their efforts. It was this drive for bright ideas that led to the development of LED TV and wireless broadband.

Samsung's future

Samsung phones on display in a shop in Thailand.

Nothing is guaranteed in the fast-moving electronics businesses. Even market leaders can sink into crisis. The industry may change, leaving them behind while newcomers enter the market and forge ahead. In 2014, Samsung was faced with slowing demand and increased competition in the smartphone industry, and profits fell. The company needs to innovate constantly to survive. What could Samsung do to keep up its global position?

Samsung hasn't acquired as many other companies as its competitors. To adopt new technologies and products, it could invest more in other companies. A good way to foster innovation is to employ a wide range of employees with different skills. Experts have pointed out that the company increasingly hires more women, young and international workers, but it could do more in this area, and give them more responsibility.

More importantly, Samsung could work towards being a Total Solution Provider, providing customers with integrated (well-linked) systems. It has created excellent products, such as MPEG-4 (a way of making small files for sending video and images), digital TV and IMT-2000 (mobile telecommunication standards for 3G mobile services), all of which were chosen for use worldwide. It introduced Tizen, its own operating system, on smartphones in 2014.

Business Matters
Transnational companies (TNCs)

Samsung is a multinational; it is based in its home country. Transnational companies have all their departments located in the best place, for example, where suitable workers live or costs are low. This may not be its home country. Yet if Samsung became a TNC, it would lose the benefits of having its divisions close together.

An exhibition hall at the Samsung Innovation Museum in Suwon, South Korea.

However, it hasn't developed its own 'platform products' – groups of software and products that have never been seen before. Apple did this by creating iTunes software and iPod music players. Yet Samsung is good at predicting trends and creating new products quickly. It developed the first graphene semiconductors and has a chance to lead the field with this breakthrough technology that could bring us a brand-new generation of must-have gadgets.

> **By 2020, we seek to achieve annual sales of USD 400 billion while placing Samsung Electronics' overall brand value among the global top 5.**
>
> **Samsung website**

market a new Samsung product

When you create a fantastic new product, you need to come up with a marketing strategy to sell it. Here's a sample marketing strategy for a possible device. Why not see if you can come up with your own idea for a Samsung product?

The Samsung Do-it-all

Building on the DigitAll idea, the Do-it-all combines all the functions of a smartphone, tablet, laptop and camera on a super-thin graphene computer that you can unroll to use wherever you are.

Stage 1 Work out your objectives

Step 1: Make sure they fit with your corporate strategy.
The Do-it-all fits perfectly with Samsung's strategy to be the first to bring out an innovative product.

Step 2: What do you hope to achieve?
Samsung's primary goal is to become the market leader. However, investing in this new technology may not bring in large profits immediately, so there are risks involved.

Stage 2 Product detail

Step 1: Product description and positioning
What is it?
The Do-it-all replaces the need for a separate computer, smartphone and camera. Made from graphene, it can be rolled out to the size of a small laptop with a keyboard, yet is as portable as a mobile. A high-quality camera is included as standard.

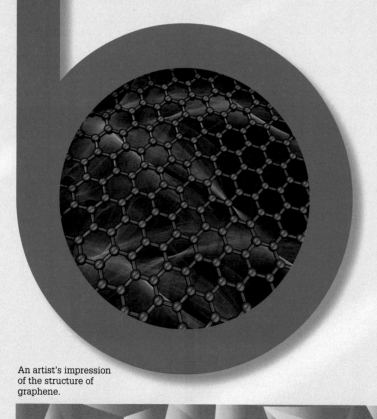

An artist's impression of the structure of graphene.

Who is it for?

People who buy top-end Samsung mobiles and fans with an interest in the latest technology.

How is it different from other products?

There is no computer or smartphone like it. If Samsung brings out the first model, it will have a huge competitive advantage.

What's the benefit?

Convenience and style: you have all your data, photos and videos on one device.

What is the evidence to support your claims?

The Do-it-all will be thoroughly tested for durability to ensure it survives being dropped on the ground, rattling around in bags and falling in water.

Step 2: What will it be used for?

It will have all the functions of laptops, smartphones and digital cameras.

Step 3: How will it be different from other products?

No other product will offer so many functions in such a light format. It will be packaged in a unique case so that it can be carried in its rolled-up form.

Step 4: What is the pricing policy?

Samsung's aim will be to enhance the perception of the brand as a leader in innovation. In keeping with Samsung's general policy, prices will be high to reflect the quality of the product.

Step 5: What's the USP?

It is the first product of its kind.

Stage 3 Understand the market

Step 1: Work out which niche gives the best sales possibilities

At first, this premium-quality, high-priced product will be sold in the wealthiest markets with the most advanced technology, such as Japan, South Korea, the USA, Australasia and Europe.

Step 2: Create customer profiles

Market research will identify target customers by focusing on the profile of people who buy top-end mobiles and laptops, and electronics fans.

Step 3: How will you access customers?

Feature articles will be written for the technology and electronics press and all the social media used by target customers.

Stage 4 Check the competition

What competition is there likely to be?

Other prominent electronics companies such as Google and Apple are likely to produce mobile and wearable graphene devices.

Stage 5 Build your sales plan

Step 1: Key messages

Key messages for the target audience will exploit the desirability of a graphene device on an emotional level – the opportunity to own a product at the forefront of technology – as well as the practicality and convenience of the Do-it-all.

Step 2: Promotion

The promotion strategy will include advertising in the press, TV, cinemas and billboards. Samsung's public relations team will offer information about the Do-it-all. A Do-it-all website and a huge social media and mobile marketing campaign will be set up, and there will be promotions to engage customers, including competitions to win the new device.

Stage 6 Launch!

High-profile launch events involving celebrities will be held in all key target markets, timed for the pre-Christmas period to encourage the highest levels of sales.

glossary

analogue
An electronic process used before digital processing.

application – 'app' for short
A program designed to do a particular job.

biotechnology
The use of living cells and bacteria in industrial and scientific processes.

Chief Executive Officer (CEO)
The person at the top of a business.

component
One of several parts of which something is made.

corrupt
When someone uses their power to do dishonest or illegal things in return for money or to gain an advantage.

digital
An electronic process using a system of receiving and sending information as a series of ones and zeros.

division
A large and important unit or section of an organization.

electronics
Equipment that uses electronic technology, with many small parts, such as microprocessors and memory chips, which control and direct a small electric current.

facility
A place, usually including buildings, used for a particular purpose or activity.

graphene
The strongest, lightest and thinnest material known.

initiative
A new plan for dealing with a problem or achieving a purpose.

innovation
The introduction of new things, ideas or ways of doing something.

investment
Putting money into a business in the hope of making more money.

liquid crystal display (LCD)
A way of showing data in electronic equipment. An electric current is passed through a special liquid, and numbers and letters can be seen on a small screen.

manufacturing
The business or industry of producing goods in large quantities in factories.

marketing
The activity of presenting, advertising and selling a company's products in the best possible way.

memory chip
A chip that holds data. RAM chips hold data temporarily while flash memory chips hold data permanently.

mentor
To advise and train someone with less experience.

microprocessor
A small unit of a computer that has the instructions for computer programs.

operating system
The 'go between' that communicates between the software programs and the hardware (the parts of the computer) to make the computer work.

premium
High quality.

random access memory (RAM)
Computer memory in which data can be changed or removed and can be looked at in any order.

revenue
The money a company earns from the sale of goods and services.

scandal
An event that people think is morally or legally wrong and causes public feelings of shock or anger.

semiconductor
A device containing a solid substance that conducts electricity in particular conditions, used in electronics.

share/shareholder
A company is divided into many equal units called shares. People can buy shares to own part of the company and receive a part of the profits – they are called shareholders.

software
The programs that run on a computer.

sponsor
A company that pays towards a radio or television programme or sporting event, usually in return for advertising.

warranty
A written agreement in which a company selling something promises to repair or replace it if there is a problem within a particular period of time.

How electronics businesses can build their brand

Make sure your customers have a positive experience with your product and address any problems straight away.

Focus on product design, giving your products the same distinctive features, such as the colour, feel and sound.

Have one master brand rather than many separate brands.

Emphasize the benefits that the products bring to people's lives.

Focus your marketing messages on your flagship (top) products.

Deliver your message through the right channels for the target market, depending on the kind of media they access.

Make sure your product names and logos are suitable in different countries.

Check there is a market for your products.

Ensure you can deliver your product reliably to your target market.

websites

Facts about Samsung
www.businessinsider.com/
mind-blowing-facts-about-samsung-2013-4?op=1
Samsung's website
www.samsung.com/uk/home

A
advertising 13, 20, 29
Apple 4, 5, 14, 19, 23, 27, 29
apps 20

B
biosimilars 19
brand affection 20
brand value 5, 17, 27

C
chaebols 7
convergence products 14
co-opetition 25
Creative Labs (C-Labs) 25

D
digital convergence strategy 19
diversification 19

E
economy pricing 15
environment 23
Everland 18, 19

F
Facebook 23

G
Galaxy 4, 19, 20, 23, 25
graphene 4, 27, 28, 29
growth 6, 16, 17

H
high-value goods 14

I
Interbrand 5

K
Kim, Eric 14, 16, 17

L
Launching People 20
Lee, Byung-Chull 6-7
Lee, Jae-Yong 19
Lee, Kun-Hee 8, 10, 19

M
marketing 14, 15, 17, 23, 29

Matsushita 16
memory chips 4, 5, 7, 11, 12
microprocessors 7, 13

N
Nokia 19

O
Olympics 20-21

P
Philips 16
planned obsolescence 22
ppali ppali 25
price skimming 14
profits 14, 17, 26, 28
public relations (PR) 8, 9, 29

R
relocation 18
research and development (R&D) 11, 24, 25
restructuring 19
revenue 4

S
semiconductors 7, 8, 13, 27
shares 18, 19
silicon chips 7
smartphone 4, 5, 23, 26, 28-29
social media 23, 29
Sony 5, 16-17, 19

T
Tizen 26
Total Solution Provider 26
Transnational Companys (TNCs) 26

U
ultra high definition TV 4, 14

W
WiBro 5

Y
Yun, Jong-Yung 10

First published in Great Britain in 2015 by Wayland

Copyright © Wayland, 2015

All rights reserved.
Dewey Number: 338.7'621381-dc23
ISBN: 978 0 7502 9264 1
Ebook ISBN: 978 0 7502 9265 8
10 9 8 7 6 5 4 3 2 1
Printed in China

FSC

Wayland
An imprint of Hachette Children's Group
Part of Hodder & Stoughton
Carmelite House
50 Victoria Embankment
London EC4Y 0DZ
An Hachette UK Company
www.hachette.co.uk

www.hachettechildrens.co.uk

Editor: Elizabeth Brent
Designer: Grant Kempster

Picture Credits: Cover: Caro/Photoshot (left), Kobby Dagan / Shutterstock.com (right); p4: Zeynep Demir/Shutterstock.com; p5: Ivan Garcia/Shutterstock.com; p6: Patrick Robert/Sygma/CORBIS (top), Mohumed Maaidh/Wikicommons; p7: Janet Wishnetsky/CORBIS (right); p8: JUNG YEON-JE/AFP/Getty Images; p9: AirTeamImages (top), TakeStockPhotography/Shutterstock.com (bottom); p10: Sean Gallup/Getty Images (top), LEE JAE-WON/AFP/Getty Images (bottom); p11: Dimas Ardian/Getty Images, Stefan Chabluk (bottom); p12: Michel Setboun/Corbis (top), CHOO YOUN-KONG/AFP/Getty Images (bottom); p13: TopFoto/ImageWorks; p14: Gilles Mingasson/Hulton Archive/Getty Images; p15: Kobby Dagan/Shutterstock.com; p16: JUNG YEON-JE/AFP/Getty Images (top), REX/Sipa Press (bottom); p17: Kobby Dagan/Shutterstock.com; p18: Tanjala Gica/Shutterstock.com (top), JUNG YEON-JE/AFP/Getty Images (bottom); p19: SeongJoon Cho/Bloomberg via Getty Images; p20: Kumar Sriskandan/Alamy; p21: Fred Duval/FilmMagic; p22: Helga Esteb/Shutterstock.com; p23 REX/Image Broker; p24: JEON HEON-KYUN/epa/Corbis (top), Kobby Dagan/Shutterstock.com (bottom); p26: Tooykrub/Shutterstock.com, p27: www.exynox.net; p28: LAGUNA DESIGN/Science Photo Library/Corbis

The author would like to acknowledge these sources:
Samsung Electronics and the Struggle for Leadership of the Electronics Industry by Anthony Michell (Wiley, 2010); *The Samsung Way: Transformational Management Strategies from the World Leader in Innovation and Design* by Professors Jaeyong Song and Kyungmook Lee (McGraw-Hill, 2014)

The diagrams on pp. 5, 11 and 24 are adapted from *The Samsung Way*.

DISCOVER THE INCREDIBLE STORIES OF THE BUSINESSES BEHIND THESE WORLD-FAMOUS BRANDS

978 0 7502 9264 1

978 0 7502 9261 0

978 0 7502 9252 8

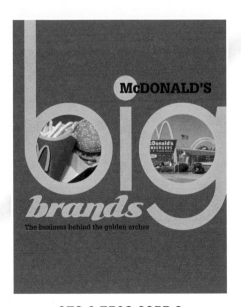

978 0 7502 9255 9